BE THE WAVE
Rise, Radiate, Revolutionize

*A Woman's Guide To
Bold Leadership and
Entrepreneurial Success*

Patricia Lynne Price

TESTIMONIALS/ SUCCESS STORIES

Linda informed her father that she wanted to be a beautician while still in high school. After going to beauty school, her father changed her bedroom into a beauty salon, and she got married and moved to her husband's farm. She was 19. She quickly expanded to having 2 more shops, employing as many as 6 other beauticians. She was able to retire at 73 and is still in her home at 82. When asked about how life as an entrepreneur was for her, Linda shared, "I would not have done it any other way. I dedicated my life to helping elderly women look their best. I was also able to volunteer at the local nursing homes one day a week. I kept my prices in line with the budget of my clientele, and I was always busy."

Sue was a second-line manager with aspirations of moving up the corporate ladder at a subsidiary of AT&T. However, after being overlooked for promotion many times, Sue jumped at the opportunity to become an entrepreneur. Sue took her knowledge as an engineer, and after being on the team to install voicemail across the country, she saw a niche that was not being filled. She was able to start her own company to do personal phone answering for local businesses, which included buying her own switch. She saw that many businesses wanted that personal touch, something the electronic voicemail sorely lacked. Sue is a very successful entrepreneur.

CONTENTS

Author   **61**

INTRODUCTION

Setting the Scene: An Overview of Today's Female Entrepreneurs and Leaders

The purpose of this book is to guide, inspire, and empower women to tap into their potential, tackle challenges, and succeed in business and life. Let's start by looking at some hard truths and inspirational stories that resonate with what you might be going through. This isn't just a guide; it's a call to action for you— the woman shifting from manager to leader, ready to make waves in the entrepreneurial world. We'll begin by understanding the landscape that many women entrepreneurs and leaders navigate, pinpoint the specific hurdles we face, and show you how this book will help turn those challenges into stepping stones for success.

The Current Landscape

In the business world today, women are more present than ever, but we are still not where we need to be at the top. While we make up nearly half the workforce, the higher you look, the fewer of us there are. The journey of a female entrepreneur or leader is fraught with unique challenges—from systemic biases to stereotypes that doubt our abilities. The obstacles are real but not unbeatable.

Unique Challenges

You've told me about feeling isolated in leadership roles, the scarcity of mentors, and the constant juggling between your career drive and personal life. Here's what we're up against:

- **Voice and Visibility**: It's tough to find a spot in decision-making circles where your voice is not only heard but valued.

- **Access to Resources**: It's often harder for us to secure funding or support due to limited networks and persistent gender biases.

- **Balancing Multiple Roles**: Managing leadership roles and personal life can often lead to burnout if we don't have the right strategies or support.

These are serious challenges, but they are not insurmountable.

The Purpose of This Book

"Be the Wave: Rise, Radiate, Revolutionize" isn't just about inspiration; it's a practical guide to navigate the often complex landscape of business leadership for women.

- **Guiding Your Path**: This book will be your roadmap, filled with actionable strategies specifically tailored to tackle the unique challenges and opportunities you face.

- **Inspiring Your Ascent**: You'll read stories of women who've broken through these barriers, providing not just inspiration but tangible proof that these obstacles can be your stepping stones to greater success.

- **Empowering Your Success**: We're talking real tools here—how to make smarter decisions, leverage your strengths, face challenges boldly, and build networks that support you. It's also about resilience: how to bounce back and keep moving forward.

Making It Personal

This journey is yours, and this book respects that. It aligns its lessons with both your personal aspirations and professional ambitions, ensuring that your growth in business enriches not just your career but also your life.

"Be the Wave: Rise, Radiate, Revolutionize" is more than a book; it's a companion for your journey to becoming a leader who doesn't just fit into the future but helps shape it. Every page you turn is a step towards realizing your vision of leading with innovation, influence, and integrity. Let this book guide, inspire, and empower you to unlock the full potential of your leadership abilities. Together, we'll embark on this journey of transformation and triumph. Let's dive in and make some waves.

Free Resource

I created a Fear and Doubt Management Plan to help you navigate through some of the challenges you are likely to face as you embark on your journey. Go to https://acalmerwave.com/free-resource to get your free copy

CHAPTER 1:
THE POWER OF INTUITION IN BUSINESS

Welcome to **"Be the Wave: Rise, Radiate, Revolutionize."** In this first chapter, we're diving into one of your most natural assets—intuition. Here, we'll explore how intuition can be a crucial tool in your leadership arsenal, helping you make complex decisions and lead with both empathy and impact.

Understanding Intuition

Often called a 'gut feeling,' intuition is your subconscious or Higher Self pulling together insights from your past experiences and current surroundings to help you make quick, insightful judgments. For us in the business world, this skill is golden because it melds emotional intelligence with hard data, letting you respond quickly to ever-changing situations. It's about trusting your inner voice to guide you through unclear times, especially when complete data isn't available.

Cultivating Your Intuitive Skills

To really tap into your intuition, try these practical steps:

- Reflect on Past Successes: Think about times when your gut led to good outcomes. What happened? What can you learn from these moments?

- Practice Mindfulness and Meditation: These methods can fine-tune your sensitivity to those intuitive nudges by quieting the mental noise that can cloud your judgment.

- Embrace Uncertainty: Be bold in making decisions even when you don't have all the pieces. Intuition often shines in unknown territory.

- Seek Diverse Feedback: Chat about your intuition-driven decisions with mentors or peers. Their perspectives can help you see if your instincts are on the money.

Intuition in Action

Take Leah, a marketing director who launched a big campaign despite iffy market data and a split team. By trusting her deep-seated knowledge and subtle customer hints, her gut decision not only smashed expectations but also set new standards in her industry.

Balancing Intuition with Analytics

Top business leaders know how to balance instinct

with thorough data analysis. This balance is key for informed decisions, letting intuition add to insights from data while analytics check the biases that can sneak into our gut feelings.

- Balanced Decision-Making: Understand when to rely on gut feelings and when you really need to dig into the data.

- Intuitive Leadership: Using your intuition can deeply enhance your leadership, especially in understanding team dynamics and leading effectively.

Why Intuition Matters in Business

Intuition does more than just guide you; it's an internal compass, especially valuable in situations where data alone just doesn't cut it. It uses your past experiences and emotional insights to let you make quick and deep decisions.

Strengthening Your Intuitive Edge

Boosting your intuition means intentionally weaving it into your everyday decisions:

- **Mindful Quieting**: Regular quiet time, like meditation or peaceful walks, helps clear the mental clutter, letting your deeper insights shine through.

- **Decision Tracking**: Keep a journal of major business decisions, the thoughts behind them, how you felt, and the results. This helps you refine your instincts over time.

- **Reflective Practice**: After going with your gut, take time to think over how effective it was. Understanding when and why your intuition was right (or wrong) builds your confidence and decision-making skills.

Practical Example: Anita's Expansion Decision

Consider Anita, who owns a boutique. Faced with a big decision about expanding her business amidst mixed signals, she reflected on subtle market trends and her own experiences. Trusting her intuition, she went ahead with the expansion, tapping into a new market trend ahead of the data, leading to great success.

Integrating Intuition with Data

The best decisions come from a harmony between intuition and data analysis. Use your gut to sense the most likely scenarios and then use data to refine and support these insights.

Strategies to Enhance Your Intuitive Skills

- **Incorporate Mindfulness**: Start with daily meditation to clear mental clutter.

- **Keep a Decision Journal**: Track the intuition involved in key decisions and their outcomes.

- **Practice with Low-Risk Decisions**: Build confidence by starting small.

- **Seek Feedback**: After making intuitive decisions, discuss them to gain insights.

Developing and trusting your intuition is more

than just improving your decision-making skills—it transforms how you lead and manage your business. These strategies are here to help you recognize and sharpen your intuitive abilities and seamlessly integrate them with analytical thinking for sound business strategies.

As we continue this journey, remember that enhancing your intuition is a step towards becoming a more insightful and effective leader. Let's keep rising, radiating, and revolutionizing as we unlock the full potential of your business intuition. Let's get started on making those smart, gut-driven decisions.

CHAPTER 2: OVERCOMING FEAR, WORRY, AND DOUBT

Fear, worry, and doubt are emotional roadblocks that can stall even the most driven leaders. In this section, we tackle these roadblocks. Here, you'll find practical strategies to help you move past these barriers and approach your business and leadership goals with renewed confidence.

Understanding Emotional Barriers

Fear, worry, and doubt often act as our natural guardians, but they can turn into roadblocks if we let them take control. In business, these feelings might show up as hesitancy to take necessary risks or anxiety over potential outcomes. It's important to recognize and understand where these feelings come from to effectively overcome them.

Identifying Your Triggers

Let's start by figuring out what exactly triggers your fear, worry, and doubt:

- **Fear**: Is it fear of failure, fear of the unknown, or fear of loss?

- **Worry**: Does your worry come from not meeting expectations or uncertainty about the outcomes of new ventures?

- **Doubt**: Do you doubt your abilities, your knowledge, or your potential to succeed?

Knowing what triggers these emotions is your first step towards tackling them.

Strategies to Master Your Emotions

- **Embrace and Analyze Your Feelings**: Actively acknowledge and think about your feelings without judging yourself. Understanding them reduces their control over you and empowers you to manage them better.

- **Cultivate a Growth Mindset**: Instead of fearing failure, view each challenge as a chance to learn and grow. This mindset helps build resilience and keeps you looking at the bright side, which is crucial for navigating business uncertainties.

- **Set Incremental Goals**: Divide big tasks into smaller, manageable steps. Celebrate every little win along the way. This strategy keeps overwhelming feelings at bay and builds a positive track record of success.

- **Practice Success Visualization**: Regularly picture yourself achieving your goals and overcoming challenges successfully. This not only prepares your mind for success but also boosts your self-confidence.

- **Create a Supportive Network**: Surround yourself with supportive peers, mentors, and allies. Having people who encourage your growth can lessen doubts and lift your spirits through both praise and constructive feedback.

- **Incorporate Mindfulness Techniques**: Use meditation, yoga, or deep breathing exercises to handle stress and anxiety daily. These practices keep your mind calm and focused, enhancing your ability to face emotional challenges head-on.

Highlighting a Success Story

Meet Elena, who tackled significant doubts when starting her own business. Elena gained the confidence she needed to face bigger challenges by first setting and achieving small goals, which eventually led to the success of her business.

Mapping the Emotional Landscape

The path to leadership is often obscured by emotional barriers that can slow us down. Acknowledging and naming these fears and doubts is your first step towards breaking them down. Here, we outline common fears that resonate with many women in the workplace:

- **Fear of Failure**: Often coming from perfectionism and high expectations, this fear might stop you from stepping into new or risky ventures, limiting both growth and innovation.

- **Fear of Invisibility**: Many women fear that their contributions will be overlooked, especially in male-dominated fields. This fear can hold you back from speaking up and sharing your ideas.

- **Imposter Syndrome**: This widespread issue can make highly accomplished women feel like they're just faking it, which can shake your confidence and stop you from taking proactive career steps.

Strengthening Your Confidence Foundation

Building confidence comes from intentional actions and positive feedback. Here are exercises and affirmations to boost your self-belief and help you tackle professional challenges successfully:

- **Power Posing**: Before important meetings, stand in a posture of confidence for two minutes to boost your assertiveness.

- **Visualization Techniques**: Regularly imagine successful outcomes in your professional tasks. This prepares your mind for success.

- **Skill Mastery**: Focus on essential skills for your role and continuously improve them through training or mentorship.

- **Challenge Yourself Regularly**: Set small challenges that push you out of your comfort zone to build a track record of success.

Dealing with fear, worry, and doubt is key to growing as a leader. By using these strategies, not only can you overcome emotional hurdles, but you also set the stage for a leadership style characterized by confidence and resilience. As you progress, let each strategy empower you to face challenges boldly and seize opportunities with both hands. Keep rising, radiating, and revolutionizing, turning your emotional barriers into stepping stones for success. Now, let's embark on the next chapter with renewed determination and clarity.

CHAPTER 3: FOSTERING A CAN-DO ATTITUDE

A can-do attitude isn't just about seeing the glass as half full; it changes the way you handle bumps in the road and really shines through in your leadership style. In this chapter, we're diving into something really crucial both in and out of the office—keeping a positive mindset.

The Real Deal on Positivity

Being positive is more than just smiling through tough times; it's a practical strategy that builds up your resilience, fires up your creative spark, and makes you a better leader. It's all about managing setbacks with a cool head and focusing on solutions, which is key for anyone looking to lead with dynamism.

Simple Steps to Stay Positive

- **Start with Gratitude:** Kick off or wrap up your day by listing three things you're thankful for. This could range from a win at work to the small joys of daily life. This shifts your focus from what's missing to what's plentiful, reducing negative vibes and boosting your overall happiness, which spills over into your work life.

- **Reframe Challenges:** When you hit a roadblock, treat it as a chance to grow. Ask yourself, "What can I learn here?" Viewing hurdles as learning opportunities eases their toll on you and improves your flexibility in handling them.
- **Keep Optimism in Check:** Regularly check and tweak your inner talk. Swap out "I can't do this" with "I'll figure it out." Keeping an optimistic outlook is not just good for the soul; it's good for your health and your success rate. It sets you up to expect—and achieve—good outcomes.
- **Mindfulness Matters:** Integrate simple mindfulness exercises like focused breathing or a quick meditative walk into your day. Mindfulness eases stress and anchors you in the now, helping you dodge overthinking about past or future hang-ups.
- **Choose Positive Company:** Make time for folks who carry a positive vibe—mentors, coworkers, and pals who lift you up. The energy of the people you hang around with can really affect your mood and outlook, giving your positivity a boost.

Real-Life Proof: Clara's Journey

Clara, who runs a tech startup, is a prime example of positive power in action. Even with the rollercoaster ride of startup life, her dedication to staying grateful and seeing the bright side has helped her steer through tough times with grace. Her positive energy doesn't just keep her going; it draws in clients and investors who are eager to work with someone who radiates such good vibes.

The Wide-Ranging Impact of Positivity

Embracing positivity can transform every facet of your professional life, from dealing with challenges to building relationships with colleagues and customers. Here's how positivity really makes a difference:

Boosting Brain Power and Connections

- **Creativity and Innovation**: Positivity broadens your thinking, helping you see beyond the usual routes and come up with fresh ideas.

- **Decision-Making**: A positive mind cuts through the panic and haste that can fog your thinking, allowing for smarter, clearer decisions.

- **Team Dynamics**: A positive approach helps create a supportive team environment that enhances cooperation and collective problem-solving.

- **Networking**: Positivity makes you magnetic, helping you grow a strong circle of contacts that can propel your career forward.

Keeping Your Cool in the Hot Seat

- **Resilience**: Viewing setbacks as temporary

bumps in the road keeps your spirits up and your goals in sight.

- **Stress Reduction**: Seeing challenges as manageable keeps stress at bay and prevents burnout, which is vital for keeping your leadership strong and steady.

Staying Positive in the Thick of It

- **Breathing Exercises**: Quick breathing sessions can calm your nerves and clear your head.

- **Positivity Journaling**: Reflect on the good stuff at the end of the day—it helps keep your focus on the wins, no matter how small.

- **Cut the Negativity**: Be selective with what you read and discuss. Stick to what uplifts and supports your goals.

- **Get Moving**: Regular physical activity boosts your mood and can be a great way to shake off work stress.

- **Affirmations and Visualization**: Use affirmations that resonate with your strengths and imagine yourself succeeding in tough scenarios.

Example of Excellence: Alex's Steady Hand

Meet Alex, a project manager who kept his cool and kept his team motivated through a challenging project by sticking to his positive practices like focused breathing and jotting down the upsides daily. His ability to stay composed under pressure not only got them through but also set a powerful example for his team.

Developing a positive mindset is key to leading well and making an impact in today's fast-paced world. By weaving positivity into your daily routines, you ready yourself for whatever comes your way and pave the way for innovative leadership and transformative growth. These strategies do more than just ease stress—they boost your ability to inspire and lead, fostering a tough, positive team spirit.

So, let's pledge to keep growing and innovating, using positivity to turn potential stumbling blocks into stepping stones for leadership and personal growth.

CHAPTER 4: MASTERING TRANSFORMATION AL LEADERSHIP

This chapter delves into transformational leadership —a real game-changer that not only propels your organization to new heights but also genuinely enhances the growth and development of your team. This style of leadership is all about inspiring and motivating your crew in a way that brings about profound, positive changes.

Understanding Transformational Leadership

Transformational leadership is all about making a positive impact on your followers. It's for leaders who are proactive, motivating, and not afraid to shake things up. This style is all about helping your team members reach their full potential, which, in turn, boosts the whole organization. Here are the four main pillars:

- **Idealized Influence**: You're the role model, setting a high bar that others are drawn to follow.

- **Inspirational Motivation**: You craft and communicate a vision that captures the imagination and fires up your team.

- **Intellectual Stimulation**: You challenge the status quo and encourage your team to think outside the box and innovate.

- **Individualized Consideration**: You take the time to mentor and support each team member's personal growth and development.

Effective Strategies for Transformational Leadership

- **Crafting and Sharing a Vision:** Develop a vision that meshes the organization's goals with the aspirations of your team. Keep the message clear and inspiring. A strong, shared vision pulls everyone together, driving collective effort toward common goals.

- **Encouraging Innovation:** Push your team to think differently and experiment. Reward both successes and valuable lessons from failures. Impact: This builds a robust team culture that's adaptable and creative, ready to face new challenges.

- **Supporting Growth:** Spot and cultivate the unique talents and ambitions within your team. Offer training, challenging assignments, or mentorship. Tailored support boosts job satisfaction and performance, which are key for keeping your team engaged and on board.

- **Leading by Example:** Walk the talk. Show integrity and accountability in everything you do, setting the standard for others. This approach not only builds trust but also establishes behavioral benchmarks for your team.

Real-Life Example: Maria's Transformational Journey

Maria, head of a department, really turned things around by leaning into transformational leadership. She set a clear vision for integrating cutting-edge technology to improve processes. By encouraging her team to own new projects and innovate, she not only boosted output but also enhanced teamwork and morale.

Why This Matters for Women in Leadership

Transformational leadership plays to many strengths typically associated with women, like empathy, nurturing, and teamwork. It's a powerful way for women to lead effectively and authentically, breaking through barriers and gaining recognition.

How Women Can Harness Transformational Leadership

- **Articulate Your Vision**: Link your personal values with organizational goals. Communicate passionately to inspire your team.
- **Foster Openness**: Build a culture where new ideas are welcomed and everyone feels valued. This encourages innovation and engagement.

- **Personalize Your Approach**: Pay attention to individual team members' needs and goals. Mentor them and align opportunities to help them grow.
- **Set an Example**: Show commitment and integrity in all you do. Your actions inspire your team to emulate these qualities.

Key Takeaways for Transformational Leadership

To really embody transformational leadership, you need to:

- **Inspire with a Vision**: Develop and communicate a vision that motivates and unites your team.
- **Foster Creativity**: Encourage innovative thinking and problem-solving.
- **Support Your Team**: Understand and cater to the individual developmental needs of your team members.
- **Emphasize Learning**: Keep pushing for personal and team growth through continuous learning opportunities.
- **Lead with Empathy**: Show you care about your team not just as workers but as people.

Nina's Story: Leading with AI

Consider Nina, who led a tech project that integrated AI to enhance efficiency and staff skills. Her commitment to innovation and personal growth within her team resulted in significant gains for the company.

Transformational leadership is essential for anyone aiming to make a significant impact in their field and within their teams. It fosters an environment of growth, innovation, and integrity. By adopting these practices, you not only boost your own leadership skills but also empower your team and pave the way for meaningful changes in your organization.

Embrace these principles to transform challenges into opportunities and drive true success. Let's keep pushing the boundaries, rising, radiating, and revolutionizing the way we lead.

CHAPTER 5: BUILDING YOUR VISION WITH CLARITY AND PURPOSE

Welcome to a crucial part of our journey in "Be the Wave: Rise, Radiate, Revolutionize." This chapter dives into crafting a vision that doesn't just echo your deepest values but also fires up and rallies your team towards a common, successful future.

The Backbone of Leadership: A Clear Vision

A clear and compelling vision is the cornerstone of effective leadership. It anchors your team, aligning everyone's efforts and guiding you through the complexities of growing an organization.

How to Create a Vision That Moves Mountains

- **Start with What Matters:** Dig deep to

identify what truly drives you. What values do you hold dear? Weave these into the vision you're building. A vision that's grounded in your genuine personal and organizational values resonates stronger and sustains commitment.

- **Know Your People:** Connect with your team, customers, and other stakeholders to grasp their needs and dreams. A vision that mirrors and tackles the aspirations and challenges of your stakeholders will likely be adopted and pursued passionately.

- **See the Future Clearly:** Picture the best possible outcome your organization aims to achieve. What does it look like? What impact does it have? Visualizing a specific, exciting future makes it easier to communicate and rally people around it.

- **Speak Simply and Clearly:** Put together a straightforward, easy-to-understand vision statement. Cut the jargon. When your vision is clear and easy to grasp, it sticks. It becomes a powerful touchstone for all organizational strategies.

- **Keep the Message Alive:** Constantly talk about the vision. Link back to it with stories of success and everyday actions. Keeping the vision front and center ensures it stays relevant and at the top of mind, helping to maintain focus and drive toward goals.

Example from the Field: Jasmine's Green Vision

Consider Jasmine, a CEO in the renewable energy sector.

She crafted a vision that positioned sustainability not just as a strategy but as a global must-do. By clearly communicating this vision and making it a core part of all company operations, she not only advanced her company's tech innovations but also rallied her team to top performance in the industry.

Aligning Your Vision with Your Values: A Step-by-Step Guide

- **Reflect on Your Core Values:** Truly understanding your values ensures your vision is more than words—it's a reflection of who you are as a leader. Think about what's truly important to you. How have these values shaped your life, and how can they guide your leadership?
- **Include Your Team:** When people see their input reflected in the vision, they're more likely to buy in and push hard to make it a reality. Use meetings, surveys, or workshops to involve your team in the vision-building process. This ensures the vision resonates widely and incorporates diverse perspectives.
- **Paint a Picture of the Future:** A clearly articulated future state not only motivates but also acts as a beacon guiding strategy and daily actions. Combine insights from your reflection and stakeholder input to outline a vibrant future state for your organization.
- **Check Alignment:** Regularly review your vision to ensure it stays true to the core values you've set. A vision that aligns with your values not only

helps steer through tough choices but also boosts your authenticity and trust as a leader.

- **Communicate and Act on Your Vision:** Make your vision a living part of your organization. Talk about it, make decisions that reflect it, and use it in evaluations and training. Keeping your vision in play ensures it molds organizational culture and keeps everyone rowing in the same direction.

Real-World Example: Carol's Community Focus

Take Carol, who leads a social enterprise. Her vision to empower local communities through sustainable practices is deeply woven into her personal value of sustainability. By articulating this vision clearly and embedding it in her operations, Carol has not only inspired her team but also attracted partners and clients who share her values, amplifying her impact.

Why a Clear Vision Matters

A well-defined vision does more than guide—it energizes and aligns your entire organization:

- **Directs and Decides**: It acts as a roadmap for decision-making, keeping efforts streamlined and effective.

- **Motivates and Engages**: It serves as a powerful motivator, enhancing job satisfaction and productivity.

- **Spurs Innovation**: It sets a stage for creativity, keeping your organization relevant and competitive.

- **Builds Trust**: Acting consistently with a clear vision enhances your credibility, making partnerships easier and more fruitful.

Living Your Vision

Develop a vision that captures your unique strengths and aspirations. Make it a part of everyday conversations, decision-making, and strategic planning. Show your commitment through actions, not just words.

Success Story: Jordan's Sustainable Leadership

Look at Jordan, who steered his manufacturing company to become a leader in sustainable practices. His clear, value-driven vision not only set new industry standards but also attracted customers and partners, boosting the company's growth and reputation.

A sharp, purpose-driven vision is more than a tool for leadership—it's the heart of your strategic approach, ensuring you and your team move forward with confidence and cohesion. Let this vision guide you, inspire change, and push everyone to reach new heights. As you refine and live out this vision, watch how it transforms not just your organization but also the broader landscape of your industry.

CHAPTER 6: STRATEGIES FOR EFFECTIVE COMMUNICATION AND COLLABORATION

Effective communication is the foundation of successful leadership. This chapter is all about mastering the crucial leadership skills of communication and collaboration. These skills are not just about sharing information—they're key to inspiring and unifying your team, creating a culture of open dialogue, and pushing everyone toward shared success.

Why Clear Communication is a Must

Effective communication is the backbone of successful

leadership. It makes sure your vision and goals are well understood, streamlines how things get done, and fosters an environment where feedback and open conversations are valued.

Boosting Your Communication Game

- **Listen Like You Mean It:** Active listening shows you value your team's input, which helps build a supportive and collaborative atmosphere. Pay full attention, repeat back what you hear to confirm understanding, and answer thoughtfully.
- **Keep It Simple and Clear:** Clear communication cuts down on mix-ups and makes your team more efficient and effective. Use straightforward language. Make sure your instructions and expectations are crystal clear.
- **Tailor Your Talk:** Customized communication boosts engagement and makes sure your message hits home as intended. Adjust how you communicate based on who you're talking to— their knowledge level, preferences, and cultural background.

Fostering a Team That Works Together Well

A top-notch team brings different viewpoints together to innovate and tackle problems more effectively, which improves project results and satisfaction across the board.

- **Encourage Everyone to Chime In:** Lead meetings where everyone gets a chance to speak up, perhaps by rotating who's in charge or using online tools for anonymous feedback. This makes sure all ideas are heard, boosting creativity and commitment—key ingredients for teamwork that really works.

- **Build Trust and Be Transparent:** Openness builds trust, crucial for a supportive and open team atmosphere that leads to success together. Share important info openly, explain your decisions, and be real about your own challenges when it makes sense.

- **Use Tools That Bring People Together:** Adopt digital tools that help with real-time collaboration and project management, no matter where everyone is located. Technology helps bridge the distance between team members, ensuring smooth cooperation and collective effort.

Example: Layla's Leadership Lifts Her Team

Look at how Layla, a marketing director, boosted her department's performance. By setting up structured team meetings focused on honest conversation and using collaborative project management tools, Layla's team grew more united, innovative, and effective.

Effective communication ensures everyone is aligned and contributes to a culture of respect and mutual trust, essential for any top-performing team.

Essential Moves for Better Communication and Teamwork

Effective communication is multi-layered and

goes beyond just exchanging information. It involves attentive listening, true understanding, and encouraging a dialogue that welcomes contributions from everyone.

- **Practice Real Listening:** When everyone feels listened to and valued, it creates an inclusive vibe that encourages diverse ideas. Listen carefully, don't interrupt, and summarize what's been said to make sure you've got it right. Push for this approach in all team interactions.
- **Be Clear and Direct:** Clear communication prevents misunderstandings and aligns team efforts, which is vital for effective action and reaching goals together. Speak plainly and avoid confusing terms, especially when assigning tasks or setting expectations.
- **Feedback That Builds Up:** Good feedback not only promotes ongoing improvement but also boosts both individual and team performance. Cultivate a feedback environment that focuses on positive reinforcement and helpful criticism. Make sure feedback is timely, relevant, and specific.
- **Use Visuals to Your Advantage:** Visual aids simplify complex info, making it easier to understand and remember, which boosts communication effectiveness. Add visuals like charts and infographics in your talks and materials. Use project management tools that visually track progress and tasks.

- **Promote Open Communication:** A culture that values open communication eases conflict resolution, supports adaptability, and nurtures a more agile team. Set up regular chances for open talks, like scheduled meetings, suggestion boxes, and casual check-ins. Lead by example with transparency.

Real-Life Success: Marcus Makes It Happen

Consider Marcus, a team leader in a global company who revamped his team's communication strategy. By starting regular strategy meetings that promote open dialogue and using a digital dashboard accessible to all, Marcus significantly improved team efficiency and morale. His commitment to clear, inclusive communication transformed a once disjointed team into a unified group known for its collaborative spirit and innovative results.

In today's complex business world, leveraging diverse perspectives isn't just the right thing to do—it's a strategic advantage.

Adopting strong communication and collaboration strategies isn't just about making work smoother—it's about building a dynamic, resilient, and innovative workforce. By applying these approaches, you create a workplace where everyone can thrive, contributing to the organization's success in a global market. This chapter lays out how to foster an environment where diversity and communication act as catalysts for success and innovation, propelling your team to new heights. Let's continue to aim high, ensuring our communication and collaborative efforts bring out the best in each of us and lead to unmatched achievements and satisfaction.

CHAPTER 7: EMBRACING SPIRITUAL AND HOLISTIC APPROACHES

Here, we explore the value of integrating spiritual and holistic practices into the business world. These approaches are crucial for creating a sustainable, fulfilling, and ethically driven work environment that supports well-being and boosts productivity.

Spirituality and Holism in Today's Business

Bringing spiritual and holistic practices into your business can transform your organization, leading to a workforce that's more engaged, motivated, and ethically driven. Here's how you can make these practices work in a professional setting.

Strategies for Spiritual Integration

- **Mindfulness and Meditation:** These practices increase focus, lower stress levels, and enhance mental health, leading to more innovative and thoughtful decision-making. Incorporate mindfulness into daily routines, like starting meetings with a brief meditation or offering mindfulness training programs.
- **Ethical and Transparent Operations:** Ethical operations foster trust and loyalty, which are vital for long-lasting relationships and a strong business reputation. Uphold high ethical standards across all business operations. Maintain openness with employees, customers, and stakeholders about company practices and decisions.
- **Purpose-Driven Objectives:** A purpose-driven approach not only unites the workforce but also attracts today's ethically conscious consumers and employees. Clearly define a mission that reflects core values and addresses wider social or environmental issues.

Incorporating Holistic Wellness Strategies

- **Promote Work-Life Integration:** Employees who feel balanced are more innovative, productive, and less likely to experience job fatigue. Support flexible work arrangements and encourage employees to engage in passions outside of work to prevent burnout.
- **Comprehensive Wellness Programs:** These programs improve overall employee well-being,

which can decrease absenteeism and boost job performance. Provide resources that support physical, mental, and emotional health, such as fitness memberships, counseling services, and wellness days.

- **Cultivate a Supportive Community:** A supportive workplace enhances a sense of belonging and commitment, improving teamwork and employee satisfaction. Create a workplace that promotes peer relationships and team support systems. Organize regular team-building activities and community service events.

Case Study: James's Holistic Leadership Approach

Consider James, the founder of a sustainable apparel company, who embraced holistic and spiritual practices at his workplace. By implementing flexible scheduling, regular wellness workshops, and a clear ethical mission, James not only improved employee well-being but also saw a surge in brand loyalty and innovation.

The Importance of Spiritual Values in Business

In business, spirituality goes beyond traditional religious meanings; it's about integrating core ethical values and a higher purpose into the company's framework. This shift significantly enhances decision-making, team dynamics, and stakeholder relationships.

Effective Approaches to Spiritual Integration

- **Establish Core Spiritual Values:** Identify

and define spiritual values that align with your personal beliefs and business ethos, such as integrity, compassion, and stewardship. These values guide all business activities, ensuring decisions and practices are ethically sound and consistent.

- **Promote Compassion and Respect:** Fostering compassion creates a supportive and inclusive workplace, increasing employee engagement and satisfaction. Develop policies and a culture that emphasize empathy, respect for diversity, and support for personal and professional growth.

- **Implement Ethical Practices:** Ethical operations build trust with consumers, attract ethically minded investors, and enhance the company's reputation. Operate transparently and uphold the highest ethical standards in all business dealings, including fair labor practices and sustainable resource use.

- **Drive Purpose-Driven Initiatives:** Purpose-driven initiatives increase employee morale and attract customers and partners who share similar values. Connect the company's mission with societal contributions, clearly showing how the business's efforts serve broader social or environmental goals.

Case Study: Carlos's Ethical Leadership

Reflect on Carlos, a founder of a renewable energy startup, who wove spiritual values into his business by prioritizing environmental sustainability and community engagement. His dedication not only fostered a positive brand image but also inspired his team and attracted significant investment.

Adopting spiritual and holistic practices in business isn't just beneficial—it's essential for fostering a thriving and supportive workplace. These methods align personal well-being with professional success, promoting a culture where both employees and the business flourish. This strategic investment not only boosts organizational effectiveness; it also instills a deep sense of ethical responsibility and contributes to a fairer, more mindful society.

Let's embrace these practices wholeheartedly, shaping our workplaces to be nurturing, dynamic, and successful environments. By leading with integrity and a profound sense of purpose, we achieve not only better economic outcomes but also a positive impact that reaches far beyond our professional spheres.

CHAPTER 8: FROM MANAGER TO BEING THE WAVE: YOUR ENTREPRENEURIAL JOURNEY

This chapter is dedicated to equipping you with the mindset, tools, and strategies necessary to navigate this transformation successfully and make a significant impact through your entrepreneurial ventures. Here, we embark on the exciting transition from managerial roles to becoming full-fledged entrepreneurs.

The Entrepreneurial Shift: From Management to Mastery

Moving to entrepreneurship means moving from executing someone else's vision to pioneering your own path. It's about taking the reins, sparking innovation, and embracing the uncertainties that come with crafting something novel.

Essential Steps for a Successful Entrepreneurial Transition

- **Vision and Goal Setting:** A well-defined, actionable vision will guide every decision and strategy, keeping you aligned with your long-term objectives. Determine what drives you and identify how you can address a market need. Visualize where you want your business to be in the next five, ten, or twenty years.

- **Strategic Business Planning:** A robust business plan is critical not only for securing funding but also for providing a structured approach to launching and growing your enterprise. Put together a comprehensive business plan that covers market analysis, operational logistics, marketing strategies, and financial projections.

- **Expanding Your Network:** A strong network offers support, advice, partnership opportunities, and insights into industry trends, all of which are invaluable. Take every chance to connect with fellow entrepreneurs, potential mentors, and industry leaders. Participate in networking events and join online communities.

- **Commitment to Lifelong Learning:** Staying educated ensures you remain competitive and adaptable to changes in your industry. Keep up with industry developments and continually enhance your skills. Look into courses, workshops, and other educational opportunities.

- **Risk Management:** Effective risk management protects your business from significant setbacks and ensures its longevity. Identify potential risks associated with your entrepreneurial venture and devise strategies to address them. This might include diversifying income streams or securing insurance.

Inspirational Entrepreneurial Stories

Consider Luca, who shifted from being a finance manager to launching a renewable energy startup. By embracing his vision, engaging deeply with the energy sector, and consistently overcoming startup challenges, Luca not only achieved business success but also made significant contributions to sustainable development.

Understanding the Transition

Transitioning from a structured corporate role to the dynamic world of entrepreneurship involves a major mindset shift. It's about becoming not just an idea generator but also a visionary who can steer these ideas to realization through strategic action and persistent effort.

Comprehensive Steps to Seamlessly Transition to Entrepreneurship

- **Conduct a Thorough Self-Assessment:** Deep self-knowledge helps you align your business concept with your strengths and passions, boosting your likelihood of success and satisfaction. Reflect on your motivations and personal goals. Evaluate your strengths and areas for development, which might include leadership skills, financial acumen, or specific industry knowledge.

- **Engage in Rigorous Market Research:** A solid understanding of the market allows you to effectively position your offering, tailor your products or services to meet market demands and stay ahead of trends. Investigate your target market to pinpoint customer needs, existing gaps, and potential competition. Utilize online resources, industry reports, and feedback from potential customers.

- **Strategize Your Financial Resources:** Strong financial planning ensures you have the necessary capital to sustain and expand your business during critical early stages. Map out your financial strategy, including initial funding, cash flow projections, and long-term financial planning. Explore various funding options, such as personal savings, loans, or venture capital.

- **Cultivate a Robust Support System:** A solid support network provides not just advice and guidance but also emotional support and potential business opportunities. Build a network of support that includes mentors, entrepreneurial peers, and industry professionals. Engage with online forums, local entrepreneurial meetups, and industry conferences.

- **Develop a Comprehensive Business Plan:** A well-prepared business plan is crucial for guiding your business development, attracting investors, and serving as a roadmap for your entrepreneurial journey. Draft a detailed business plan that includes your strategic approach, operational framework, marketing strategy, and financial forecasts.

- **Prepare for Personal and Lifestyle Adjustments:** Preparing for lifestyle changes helps reduce stress and improves your overall well-being, keeping you focused and driven towards your business goals. Plan for changes in your daily routines and personal life. Implement strategies to maintain work-life balance, manage time effectively, and reduce stress.

Inspirational Case Study: Elena's Tech Consultancy Success

Reflect on Elena's journey from a senior corporate role to founding a leading tech consultancy. Her methodical preparation, guided by a clear vision, enabled her to establish a business that not only fulfills a market need but also aligns with her personal aspirations and values.

Embracing entrepreneurship is about more than starting a business; it's a profound shift towards innovation, leadership, and responsible business practices. Equip yourself with the right strategies, embrace each challenge, and seize opportunities with enthusiasm and insight. The guidelines provided in this chapter are designed to not only prepare you for starting your business but also to inspire you to become a visionary leader who turns challenges into opportunities.

Step forward with confidence, leveraging your unique skills and insights to make a positive impact and drive change. Let's continue to rise, radiate, and revolutionize our industries, one innovative step at a time.

CONCLUSION: EMBRACING YOUR PATH TO TRANSFORMATION

This book wasn't just crafted to inform and enlighten —it's a call to inspire action, guiding you through a metamorphosis from being a leader of today to a visionary of tomorrow. Let's reflect on the transformative journey we've embarked on together

Key Concepts and Their Interconnectivity

We've journeyed through harnessing intuition, overcoming fears, fostering positivity, embracing transformational leadership, crafting clear visions, enhancing collaboration, and weaving spiritual and holistic practices into our work lives. Each chapter builds on the next, creating a robust framework for your personal and professional growth.

Why This Matters

The strategies laid out in this book are designed to equip you with the tools needed to lead not only with efficiency but also with empathy and creativity. By adopting these methods, you're preparing yourself to make a significant impact, driving changes that benefit not only your career but also those around you.

Your Action Plan

Moving forward, consider how to integrate these insights into your life:

- Reflect on each chapter's key takeaways—how do they relate to your current challenges and goals?

- Set specific, actionable goals based on these strategies to start creating small waves of change in your environment.

- Seek continuous growth through further learning, networking, and experimenting with new leadership practices.

Your Journey Forward

Equipped with a diverse toolkit, you're ready to rise, radiate, and revolutionize—whether in your current role, a new business venture, or through personal development. Let the lessons in these pages inspire you to not only dream big but also act purposefully, creating waves that propel you and those around you toward greater success and fulfillment.

Embrace this journey with the knowledge that your actions today shape the waves of tomorrow. Here's to your success as you navigate this exciting path, ready to make lasting impacts and lead with confidence and creativity. Let "Be the Wave" continue to guide and inspire you every step of the way.

In closing, don't just absorb the insights and strategies shared—act on them. This book is your springboard into a world of possibilities where your leadership and entrepreneurial dreams can become realities. Take that first decisive step today towards transforming your professional life and embracing the entrepreneurial journey. The path is set; now, it's your turn to walk it.

ABOUT THE AUTHOR

Patricia Lynne Price is an entrepreneur with many years of experience, having started several businesses. Patricia has been doing therapy for sixteen years after earning a Bachelor's Degree and a Master's Degree in Social Work. Research and growth in spirituality, training in Reiki and touch healing, iridology, and reflexology, as well as the best use of homeopathy and herbs to heal the body, have culminated in a good foundation for business and life coaching.

928-628-8708

ACalmerWave@outlook.com